Tall Ships: An Odyssey

Tall Ships

AN ODYSSEY

Harry Bruce

KEY PORTER BOOKS

Canadian Cataloguing in
Publication Data available on
request

The publisher gratefully acknowl-
edges the support of the Canada
Council for the Arts and the
Ontario Arts Council for its publishing program.

We acknowledge the financial
support of the Government of
Canada through the Book
Publishing Industry Development
Program (BPIDP) for our publish-
ing activities.

Key Porter Books Limited
70 The Esplanade
Toronto, Ontario
Canada M5E 1R2

www.keyporter.com

Cover design: Peter Maher
Photo credits: Thad Kozic: pp.30
(top), 34, 40, 54, 57, 62, 72, 79, 84
85.
All other photos courtesy of MAX

Printed and bound in Canada

00 01 02 03 04 05 6 5 4 3 2 1

Contents

Introduction by Harry Bruce 6

European Race: SOUTHHAMPTON AND GENOA TO CADIZ 18

Westbound Transatlantic Race: CADIZ TO BERMUDA 36

Cruising in Company: BERMUDA TO BOSTON 50

North American Race: BOSTON TO HALIFAX 68

Eastward Transatlantic: HALIFAX TO AMSTERDAM 86

APPENDIX

Rig Diagrams 92

The Classes 94

Ship Specifications 95

Introduction

I t is the summer of 1939, and I am five years old at Cape Cod, Massachusetts. I walk barefoot on ribs of sand, and splash about in tepid puddles that the retreating tide has left for me, and for a scuttling crab or two. I have never explored tidal flats before. Nor have I sniffed this exhilarating yet strangely tranquilizing aroma of wet seaweed, or heard the distant roar of ocean surf, or seen such blooming, towering, miraculously layered clouds. Above me, they blot out the sun, but far, far out—down a sunlit path that glitters only along the horizon—a three-masted, square-rigged ship marches over the Atlantic Ocean toward some southern destination.

Decades later, I buy a reproduction of an oil painting by that master of illustration for children, N.C. Wyeth. He was a Massachusetts man, and this work shows six boys and girls playing on a beach that's a ringer for the one I knew on that July afternoon such a long time ago. Beyond the youngsters— skyscraper-high and camouflaged by those same miraculously layered clouds—looms a long-haired giant. He wears a kind of Dark Ages tunic and studded leather belt. Though carrying a club on his right shoulder, he looks more determined than dangerous. He marches over the Atlantic Ocean toward some southern destination. Nowadays, "The Giant" hangs in one of my granddaughter's bedrooms, and whenever I see him I also see the square-rigger. The ship, too, was magical.

For others, as well, visions of windjammers under full sail have long been unshakeable. In 1910, the *Preussen* out of Hamburg—a steel ship 433 feet long, carrying 60,000 square feet of canvas, and loaded with 8,000 tons of nitrates from the west coast of South America—overtook a smaller sailing vessel from England.

"Within the hour, the overhauling ship was beside the little barque, rush-

The Khersones

ing by in a smother of foam," Alan Villiers wrote in *The Way of a Ship* (1953). "Those aboard the barque felt their ship was standing still. They saw that the [*Preussen*] was a five-masted full-rigged ship. She was lying over a little, with her lee scuppers awash, and the sea was gushing from her wash-ports. She was a great lofty vessel with masts 200 feet high towering upon the sea, dwarfing the barque whose astonished apprentices counted 43 sails, all set magnificently and pulling like horses....No one aboard the little *Limejuice* barque would ever forget the grace and glory of that great ship, racing past them, while they lived."

Nor would passengers aboard a British steamship bound for Rio de Janeiro in October 1934, forget the four-masted *Herzogin Cecilie*, which they saw on the South Atlantic. "Windjammer" strikes me as one of the most romantic nouns in the English language, but it started as an insult. Steamship crews derided the last of the multimasted, canvas-driven monsters as so clumsy they could not sail neatly into the wind but had to be jammed into it sideways. Now, as the steamer closed on the *Herzogin Cecilie*, the British captain chose to amuse his passengers at the expense of the oafish old barque. He would order full speed ahead, insultingly cross her bows, and then vanish over the horizon. As the steamer picked up speed, however, so did the wind. Captain Sven Eriksson ordered the *Herzogin Cecilie* to break out, and sheet home, every one of her 35 sails. Forty-five-thousand square feet of heavy canvas. With the wind hitting 40 knots—close to gale force—with her lee rail scooping green water and two crewmen wrestling with her enormous wheel to keep her on course, this senior citizen among tall ships tore along beside the steamship at better than 17 knots.

No other vessel witnessed this strange race. The 20th-century passenger liner and the throwback to the 19th century charged neck-and-neck over the empty ocean. Then the 19th century slipped ahead of the 20th. The gap widened, and kept on widening. Acknowledging defeat, the British captain blew three long blasts on his steam whistle, and dipped his red ensign in

tribute. Captain Eriksson dipped his white and blue Finnish colors, and headed for South Australia to fetch a load of grain.

Until I read about this race in *The Windjammers* (1978) by Oliver E. Allen, an American whose great-great-grandfather owned tea-clippers that sailed between Philadelphia and Canton, it never occurred to me that, as late as the year I was born, 1934, the mightiest windjammers could still sail faster than a steamship could steam. Sadly, however, it was just as centuries of improvement in the design, building, and technology of sailing vessels led them to their pinnacle of power and efficiency that the hateful "steam kettles" started to elbow them off the sea lanes of the world.

While lamenting the disappearance of the 19th century's wooden clipper ships—the fastest, sleekest, and most rakish flowerings of the age of sail— British nautical writer C. Fox Smith in 1948 called them "one of the most nearly perfect creations ever made by man for man's service." Alas, however, "All those wonderful fleets which in their day made lovely all the harbours of the world were to vanish as completely as the ice-floes in the Gulf Stream, or as one of their own fore-topsails snatched out of the bolt-ropes by the rough breath of the westerlies."

Allen was equally tearful about the windjammers that followed the clippers into oblivion. He said that even before the *Herzogin Cecilie* left the British liner in her wake, "She and all her sisters were doomed. Those who sailed the tall ships, and those who watched them pass—like all the passengers and crew of the liner on that sun-splashed October morning—knew quite well what Britain's Poet Laureate John Masefield had in mind when he wrote of the windjammers: "They mark our passage as a race of men,/ Earth will not see such ships as these again."

After World War II, the handful of windjammers still working as commercial freighters included the *Passat* and the *Pamir*. Along with the *Peking*, *Pommern*, and *Padua*, these were four-masted barques. Built in Germany in the 1920s for the famous Flying "P" Line of Hamburg, they boasted perhaps the strongest steel hulls in the history of sail. After 1950, however, not even the "P" ships continued to brave the weather horrors off Cape Horn at the tip of South America.

In 1956, London solicitor Bernard Morgan persuaded a handful of prominent yachstmen, including Earl Mountbatten, to sponsor a glorious farewell to the long-dead age of sail on the high seas. They would organize a race, from Torquay, Cornwall, to Lisbon, for the last of the great square-riggers. From Norway came the *Christian Radich* and the *Sorlandet*, from Denmark the *Danmark*, from Belgium the *Mercator*, and from Portugal the *Sagres*, all of them government-owned training vessels for sailors. Thus it was that five, enormous, sea-going anachronisms set out on a thousand-mile funeral parade for a conquered technology.

But a funny thing happened on the way to the graveyard. The funeral turned into a revival meeting. The public adored the majesty, romance, power, and sheer beauty of these towering phantoms of the past. The European press coverage of the race was extravagant and loving. After a British journalist coined "Tall Ships' Race," the phrase blossomed on front pages throughout the United Kingdom. Overnight, the idea that the first Tall Ships' race should also be the last became unthinkable. The race organizers quickly founded the Sail Training Association (now the International STA) to plan future races. A movement was born.

That handful of English yachstmen who, 44 years ago, unwittingly

Simon Bolivar from Venezuala

started it all with their grand and sentimental gesture, would have been happy to have seen one race every two years. They'd have been astounded to witness their effort blossom into an ever-growing series of annual competitions by ships from two dozen countries, races that require the formidable organizational skills of no fewer than 16 national sail training associations around the world.

In a masterful public relations coup, Cutty Sark Scots Whisky in the 1970s began to sponsor the European races that the Sail Training Association organized, and by 1996 they'd become so popular that a series on the Baltic Sea attracted no fewer than 135 vessels from 19 countries while, at the same time, 46 more ships from 11 nations competed in another Cutty Sark series on the Mediterranean. Many races, however, occur without the whisky company's backing. All in all, hundreds of Tall Ships compete every year. Thousands of young crew, speaking a score of languages, do their deep-sea duty aboard the vessels. Million of landlubbers, who don't know a sheet from a halyard, show up to applaud the Parades of Sail at the biggest cities the competitors visit.

Yet none of the series of races has ever been bigger, longer, or more challenging than this year's trans-Atlantic charges. Organized by the international and American sail training associations as "Tall Ships 2000," and billed as the Tall Ships' Race of the Century, the events began with a dozen vessels racing from Southampton to Cadiz, and a half-dozen more from Genoa to the same ancient Spanish port. The third contest saw Italian, Irish, Polish, Dutch, German, Spanish, Danish, Russian, and British vessels cross the Atlantic from Cadiz to a finish line at Bermuda.

Joining them there were tall ships from South America, Canada, the United States, and the Bahamas. By mid-June, the vessels from both sides of the Atlantic were not racing but "cruising in company." As they made their lovely and leisurely way up the east coast of the U.S., they'd drop in on Charleston, South Carolina; Annapolis, Maryland; New York, during the Independence Day celebrations of July 4; Newport, Rhode Island; and Martha's Vineyard, Massachusetts. By the time they reached Boston, the starting line for the race to Halifax, Nova Scotia, vessels from Japan and New Zealand would have caught up with the fleet. Halifax anticipated the arrival in late July of more than 100 Tall Ships. Since 40 to 50 wooden schooners from New England and Nova Scotia would join the party, the Canadian port was set to welcome perhaps the biggest gathering of sizeable sailing vessels the world had ever seen. Even the Spanish Armada numbered only 130-odd ships.

The final race would see the Tall Ships leave Halifax on July 24 and, in late August, sail triumphantly through the English Channel to the Netherlands, and the spectacular maritime festival, SAIL Amsterdam. The four-masted, 372-foot-long *Kruzenshtern* from Russia, the 101-year-old, 61-foot *Jens Krogh* from Denmark, the immaculately maintained, 132-foot *Eye of the Wind* from Britain—and all the others completing the voyages from Southampton to Cadiz, to Bermuda, to Boston, to Halifax, to Amsterdam—would have crossed the Atlantic twice in four months, and logged some 13,000 miles. The *Soren Larsen*, a British-owned brigantine, would sail 7,000 nautical miles from her home port in New Zealand to reach the Panama Canal, and after that, another 2,000 to reach the starting line in Boston. Then, she'd race to Halifax and Amsterdam, sail up the Thames to Greenwich, and prepare for a voyage back across the Atlantic, through the canal again, and on to Galapagos, Easter Island, Tahiti, Tonga, and Fiji.

By some estimates, the summer of '92 saw more than seven million people turn up at Boston, one of the most historic ports in the New World, to gawk and marvel at the Tall Ships that gathered and paraded there. Three years later at Amsterdam, the mighty square-riggers and their smaller but no less graceful relatives attracted more than a million spectators on each of four consecutive days. Even at lesser cities like Falmouth, Aberdeen, and Oporto in northern Portugal, Tall Ships' rallies have drawn crowds of half a million. With respect to attendance, these gatherings of floating throwbacks to the Victorian Era are easily the biggest sports events on the face of the globe. Admission free.

But they are far more than sports events. They are the happiest and sunniest of all international gatherings. No vessel may enter an official Tall Ships' race unless at least half her crew are between 15 and 25 years old. At the end of some races, crew trade ships to "cruise in company." For all

these thousands of boys, girls, and young men and women from myriad countries, every port the Tall Ships visit entertains crews with waterfront festivals, outdoor music, parties and fireworks. The crews return the favor by parading in uniform and behind their flags through downtown streets, and performing for the locals at "Cadet Olympics." Tall Ships' rallies are nothing less than floating world's fairs.

Few experiences build character faster than crewing on a Tall Ship. Recalling life aboard a barque of the Flying "P" Line half a century ago, Holger Thesleff wrote, "The whole crew, from captain to mess-boy, had to struggle hard when the need arose, calling upon their reserves of strength, agility, skill and presence of mind, the crew spending hour after hour up in the rigging, tearing their calloused hands on ropes and wires, or, lashed to the wheel, struggling to force the ship spoke by spoke back on to a lost course. Sails still had to be sewn and patched, bent and taken in; wires and ropes must be spliced, wormed, parceled and served; the hundreds of tackles and ropes in the rigging must be kept free to run at every change in the wind or course. Those are the jobs the sailor must do, the special tasks that only occur in sailing ships. And each man must be ready 'day and night.'"

With efficient engines, advanced meteorological briefings, and the latest navigation equipment, modern Tall Ships are no longer as hazardous as they once were, but sailing them still takes courage, teamwork, good humor, and the conviction that the well-being of everyone on board depends on your doing your job, and doing it right. "Leadership, paradoxically, is arrived at by learning to take direction," says Pamela C. Wuerth of the American Sail Training Association. "Becoming a team player. Pulling your share of the load. Being absolutely responsible. Dependable. And, learning to depend on the responsibility of others."

In *Tall Ship News*, Vice Admiral Sir George Vallings remembered sailing on Russia's fully rigged ship *Mir* during a race from Falmouth, England, to Lisbon, and how the crew reacted on a pitch-black night when the wind hit 35 knots, the rain spat horizontally, the 358-foot-long vessel heeled over sharply, and an alarm summoned all hands. Dressed only in safety harnesses and what they were wearing when the alarm rang, the crew instantly swarmed on deck.

"It took 10 minutes of amazing controlled and disciplined activity to furl eight square sails and lower four staysails," Vallings wrote. "The order was then given to go aloft and secure the eight furled but still wildly flapping square sails. Within seconds, some 50 young Russians were clambering up the rigging to the highest yards on all three masts. One was filled with admiration for the courage, athleticism and teamwork of these young men. After about 15 minutes they were all back on deck, safe and sound. Job done. It had been a hectic half hour, but the ship was still on course and still doing eight knots. The only difference was that she carried 11 rather than 26 sails."

That half hour, Vallings concluded, "will remain with me for the rest of my life."

Watching crew go aloft, stow sails, or just scrub decks and polish brass delights spectators, but some of those in the crowds must also sense the thrill of being aboard a Tall Ship when she cuts her engines and breaks out sails.

"Crew monkeyed up the rigging ratlines to spread out precariously on spars 30, 60, 90 feet up, and release great curtains of rippling canvas," recalled British writer Martin Jackson, after sailing on the *Kaskelot*, out of South Cornwall. "Tug-of-war teams scampered to haul or ease the bewildering loom of braces, halyards, clews, sheets and buntlines fencing the rails. The sails stretched into pillars of solid curves, and the ship changed character like an actor slipping into role. Suddenly, you could feel the balanced tension between the broad hull and the massive Douglas Fir masts, as she rode majestically through the waves. 'She's a living thing,' insisted second mate Nikki Alford."

About 40 of these living things raced from Bermuda to Halifax in early June, 1984. That can be a nasty part of spring in the port Rudyard Kipling

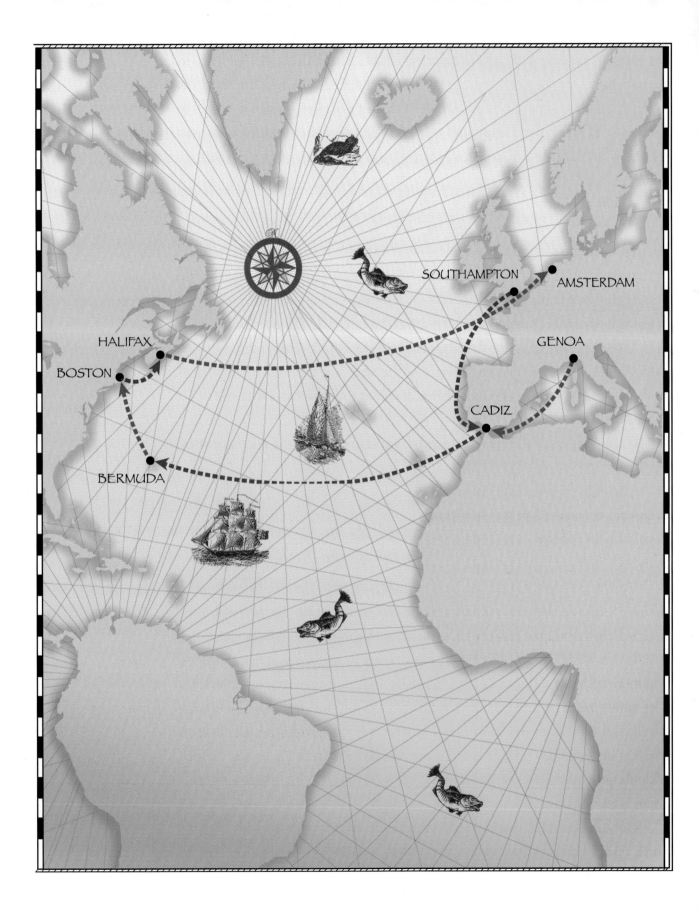

The *Alexander von Humbolt*

called "The Warden of the Honour of the North," but for five romantic and miraculous days, the weather was hot, sunny, and breezy. Tens of thousands of locals and tourists mingled with happy crews from a dozen nations. All along the waterfront, the smells of hotdogs, fish and chips, beer, perfume, and flesh, lathered with suntan oil, mingled with the sound of bagpipes, guitars, fiddles, brass bands, cheers and laughter.

On the last day, the city took the afternoon off to watch the ships make a slow, gigantic loop around the harbor, and then glide out to the open Atlantic for a race to Quebec City. Spectators packed every downtown roof, every pier, every waterfront walk and park. They clapped for each vessel as she passed, and whooped for her like country-music fans at The Grand Ole Opry. And then, too soon, the Tall Ships were gone, and there was nothing to do but remember their impossible grace. The city was forlorn.

Now, however, a fleet of Tall Ships at least three times as big as 1984's is bound for Halifax, and I'll be here to applaud every one of those big beauties. Never again will I be a boy at Cape Cod but, as the Tall Ships glide in triumph into the first summer of the new millennium, they'll make me and millions of others feel young at heart.

HARRY BRUCE

The European Races

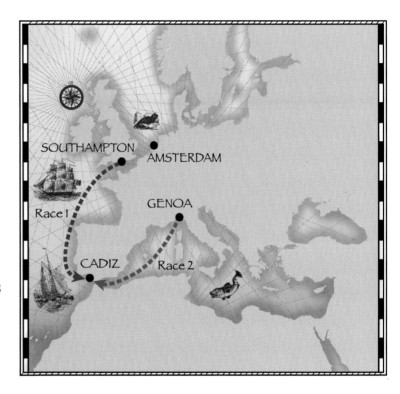

all Ships 2000 began in mid-April with races from Southampton and Genoa to Cadiz, Spain, three of the most historic seaports in the world. Southampton rightly calls itself "Gateway to the World." It was here that, almost a millennium ago, King Canute issued his legendary command to the rising tide. It was from here that Henry V left for the Battle of Agincourt, that the Pilgrim Fathers sailed for America and the Allied fleet departed for Normandy on D-Day.

Beautifully situated on the Italian Riviera, Genoa is Italy's chief seaport. It's been a port ever since navigation began, flourished in Roman times, produced no less a navigator than Christopher Columbus and has waved farewell to a slew of famous sailors.

And Cadiz? One of the oldest cities in Europe, its history goes all the way back to the Phoenician merchants. At one time, Portuguese, French, English, Scots, Irish, Flemish and Italians all integrated in Cadiz. No port could be a more appropriate spot for the two European fleets of Tall Ships to get together for a race to the New World.

Asgard II
The vessel uphold-
ing the sea-going
honor of Ireland in
Tall Ships 2000
was the nation's
only sail-training
ship in 1999, the
Asgard II. As every
good Irishman
knows, it was from
the Emerald Isle
that St. Brendan
and his sea-savvy
crew of monks
sailed in a leather
boat to mainland
North America,
and that was a
mere nine-and-a-
half centuries
before laggards
like Christopher
Columbus and
John Cabot showed
up in the New
World.

Dar Mlodziezy
The first of six
three-masted sail-
training ships that
naval architect
Zygmunt Choren
designed and the
Gdansk Shipyard
built, the *Dar
Mlodziezy* ("Gift of
Youth"), owned by
the Merchant
Marine Academy
in Gydnia, first set
sail in 1982. Since
then, she has com-
peted in most of
the Cutty Sark Tall
Ships' Races.

Europa
Launched in Hamburg, Germany in 1911, the *Europa* spent six decades as a permanently anchored lightship. She was rebuilt as a three-masted barque between 1987 and 1994, and now, nearly 90 years after she first slid down the ways, enjoys a highly varied deep-sea career.

Eye of the Wind
Built in 1923 by
C. Luhring of
Brake, Germany, to
take animal hides
from South
America to Europe;
owned for half a
century by Swedes
who had her carry-
ing general cargo
in the Baltic and
North Seas and
drifting for herring
off Iceland; origi-
nally named
Friedrich and then
Merry; ravaged by
an engine-room
fire that wrecked
her wheel house
and poop deck in
1969, the *Eye of the
Wind* has emerged
from her check-
ered history as
something very
close to a miracle.

Jens Krogh

One of the oldest Tall Ships afloat, the *Jens Krogh* was built in 1899 at the H.V. Buhl yard, Frederikshavn, north Denmark. She worked as a fishing boat for 74 years in the Kattegat around the top of Denmark and in the North Sea.

By 1973, when she stopped fishing, she was the *Ulla-Vita* and her home port was Saeby. That was where the new sailing division of Denmark's national youth organization found her. In spring and autumn, the *Jens Krogh* trains Danish and other youngsters during weekend outings, but in summer she usually divides a long summer voyage into one- or two-week legs.

(PREVIOUS PAGE)
Kruzenshtern
One of the biggest Tall Ships still sailing, the Russian training vessel *Kruzenshtern* was once the *Padua*. The last of the famous vessels of the Hamburg-based Flying "P" Line that's still sailing, she was built at Wesermunde, Germany, in 1926. The "P" ships traded in the Atlantic, Pacific and Indian oceans. On her topsides, the *Kruzenshtern* still displays the black and white, imitation gunports that the "P" line believed scared off pirates in the Far East.

28

Lord Nelson
The *Lord Nelson* takes heavy water over her port rail as a stiff wind drives her onward.

Mir

Now sporting a broad, blue band on her topsides to distinguish her from her five near-sisters, including the *Dar Mlodziezy*, Russian training ship *Mir* ("Peace"), belongs to the Admiral Makarov State Maritime Academy. Built in Poland in 1987, the *Mir* is both elegant and fast. In 1992, in the races from Cadiz to North America and back to Liverpool—to mark the Christopher Columbus quincentenary—she finished first overall. In 1996, she played host to the Cutty Sark Tall Ships' fleet at her home port, St. Petersburg, and again proved how speedy she could be. While winning the final leg of the race from Rostock, Germany to St. Petersburg, she beat all the other Class A vessels. "For speed among the large ships," according to the book *Sail to Adventure*, "she is still the one to beat in the new millennium."

Rona II

"Our aim," said Lord Amory, when he founded the London Sailing Project in 1960, "is to provide opportunity for young men to acquire those attributes of seamen, namely a sense of responsibility, resourcefulness and teamwork, which will help them throughout their lives." The Chancellor of the Exchequer of the British government at the time, he bought *Rona*, a classic, 77-foot ketch, and converted it to take a crew of 19.

Rona II normally sails to France and the Channel Islands, but in mid-summer competes in Tall Ships races.

Lord Nelson
The crew of the
Lord Nelson work
on the yard arm.

Amerigo Vespucci
The *Amerigo Vespucci* sails regularly, and captivates Tall Ships lovers in every port she visits. The Italians built her in 1931, and named her after the navigator from Florence who sailed along the east coast of the New World with Christopher Columbus from 1497–1502. Amerigo's name was the inspiration for the word "America."

The *Morning
Star of Revelation*
catching a breeze.

Kaliakra
Named after a leg-
endary Bulgarian girl
who, along with 39
others, hurled her-
self off a cliff into
stormy seas rather
than face conversion
during the Turkish
conquest of Bulgaria,
the *Kaliakra* is a
near-sister to
Poland's *Pogoria*
(opposite page). She
trains students at the
Maritime Academy,
Varma, to become
officers in the
Bulgarian merchant
fleet.

(OPPOSITE) *Pogoria*
Built in 1979–80 in Gdansk for a sail-training organization called the Iron Shackle
Fraternity, *Pogoria* promptly made her debut in a Tall Ships' race between Kiel, Germany,
and Amsterdam. Under a charter from the Polish Academy of Sciences in 1980–81, she
sailed to the Antarctic to relieve the Polish Station on King George Island. In 1982, she
competed in Tall Ships' races from Falmouth, England, to Lisbon, to Vigo in Spain and
back to Southampton. Later, she made a training voyage for young Poles right around
Africa and over to Bombay.

Westbound Transatlantic Race

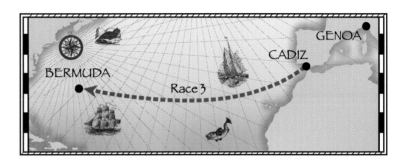

From Cadiz, the European Tall Ships raced roughly 4,000 miles to Bermuda, where, in early June, vessels from North America and South America joined them for the non-competitive "cruise in company" up the east coast of the United States to Boston. One of Britain's oldest, self-governing colonies and once an important base for the Royal Navy, Bermuda boasts such clear water, sumptuous beaches and delightful weather that Mark Twain wrote, "Some people on their way to Heaven stopped at Bermuda and thought they'd arrived." Bermuda has a population of only 56,000, but every year its charms attract nearly 10 times as many tourists.

Its safe, picturesque harbors offer excellent anchorages and berths for vessels ranging from 25-foot yachts to 700-foot cruise ships. Not a year goes by that Bermuda doesn't play host to famous ocean yacht races, and it's no stranger to the Tall Ships competitors. They visited it in 1964, 1976 and 1984.

Cadiz to
Bermuda

Asgard II
Time out for a
romp by the
bowsprit.

Bluenose II
The first *Bluenose*, which slid down the ways in Lunenburg in 1921, had two purposes: to
fish for cod off the Grand Banks of Newfoundland and to beat the fastest fishing schooners
out of Massachusetts in races for the International Fishermen's Trophy. In both roles, she
was supremely successful. She set the record for the biggest catch of fish any schooner ever
brought into Lunenburg, and her racing triumphs during the 1920s and '30s turned her
into Canada's most famous sailing vessel. She has appeared on Canadian postage stamps,
and still sails from right to left across the Canadian dime.

Concordia
West Island College International designed the *Concordia*, launched in 1992, as a floating campus. Owned by Class Afloat, a non-profit educational organization affiliated with high schools across Canada and the U.S., the *Concordia* aims to foster self-sufficiency, cooperation and awareness of foreign cultures.

Dar Mlodziezy
In 1988, while representing Poland at the celebrations marking the bicentennial of the first British settlement in Australia, the *Dar Mlodziezy* glided under the Sydney Harbor Bridge with all sails set. Scarcely three feet separated the tops of her masts and the lowest part of the bridge. Homeward-bound, she safely rounded Cape Horn during heavy weather on the most notoriously treacherous waters in the world.

Europa
The *Europa* is the official sail-training ship of the Netherlands Nautical College at Enkuizen, a port in North Holland province. She takes paying trainees on 14-day "Adventure Sailing Excursions" to France, England, Norway, Denmark, Sweden and Germany, and seven-day "Discover the Baltic" voyages from Rostock, Germany, to Sweden.

The crew of the *Gorch Frock* aloft.

Jens Krogh
Tall Ships 2000 is the *Jens Krogh's* 20th series of races in 20 years. In 1999, after a race brought her from the Shetland Islands to her home port of Aalborg for her 100th birthday, Vice Admiral Sir George Vallings wrote, "Few other vessels in the Tall Ships' fleet can match this record, which is all the more remarkable for the fact that she was 81 years old when she took part in her first race. Needless to say, she is off across the Atlantic again next year." She has now sailed in three different centuries.

Eye of the Wind
The *Eye of the Wind* visited Australia for its bicentennial celebrations in 1988 and sailed the South Pacific in 1990 to join the 200th anniversary of the settlement of Pitcairn Island by the Bounty mutineers. In 1991, she sailed from Sydney back to Europe via Cape Horn, and in 1992 raced across the Atlantic to the U.S. for Tall Ships' rallies marking the Christopher Columbus quincentenary. She has played supporting roles in the movies *Blue Lagoon, Savage Islands, Taipan* and *White Squall.*

Lord Nelson

The successful performance of the *Lord Nelson* in its mission to give the disabled a chance at the challenge of crewing on a Tall Ship has inspired Britain's Jubilee Sailing Trust to undertake construction of the *Lord Nelson II* in Woolston, Southampton. During shipbuilding holidays, disabled and able-bodied volunteers work alongside professional shipwrights to construct the new vessel.

48

Pogoria

The Canadian Educational Alternative in the late 1980s chartered the *Pogoria* full-time for use as a floating school. Since then she has sailed mostly European, Caribbean and Canadian waters. In 1933, the city of Gydnia and its sailing foundation became joint owners of the ship, along with the Polish Yachting Association, and refitted her to suit the aims of the Sail Training Association of Poland.

(PREVIOUS PAGE)
Juan Sebastian de Elcano

A training ship for Spanish naval cadets, the powerful, hard-driving *Juan Sebastian de Elcano* has circled the globe no fewer than seven times. The man from whom she takes her name was in command of the first ship to complete a circumnavigation of the world. He was captain of one of the five vessels in the five-ship fleet of explorer Ferdinand Magellan. Killed by natives in the Philippines during that epic expedition, Magellan did not make it home to Spain, but on September 6, 1522, with only a handful of men, de Elcano did.

(OPPOSITE) *Kruzenshtern*

As the German cargo ship *Padua*, the 74-year-old *Kruzenshtern* sailed to C for nitrates and Australia for wool and grain. After World War II, Russia possession of her, and named her after navigator Adam Johann von Kruzenshtern (1770–1846), surveyor of oceans and the first Russian to c cumnavigate the globe. Her owner now is the Fisheries Board of Russia, her purpose is to train Russian sailors. In 1974, she became the first Ru vessel to compete in the Cutty Sark Tall Ships' Races.

Cruising in Company

From Bermuda, Tall Ships from three continents— Europe and North and South America—sailed northeast toward Boston. During this "cruise in company," they dropped in on such ports as Charleston, South Carolina; Annapolis, Maryland; Newport, Rhode Island; and, on Independence Day, New York City. By mid-July, they'd have arrived in Boston, where the last of the Tall Ships from Japan and New Zealand would have caught up with them. No American port is more historic. Boston is where the American Revolution began, and in the nineteenth century it was home to some of the fastest and most beautiful clipper ships in the China tea trade.

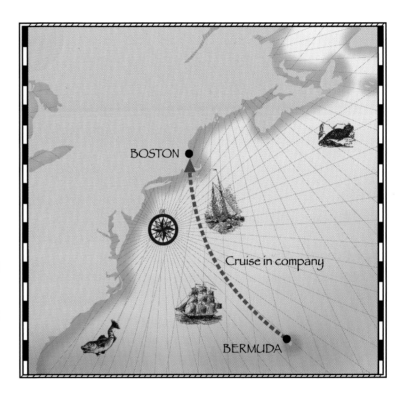

It's rich in museums, art galleries and orchestras, and its recently revitalized waterfront and downtown are ideal for entertaining sea-going officers, crew and cadets. Boston knows the Tall Ships. When they visited the port in 1992, millions of people turned out to see and applaud them.

From Boston, on July 16, the Tall Ships would race to Halifax, Nova Scotia, Canada.

Bermuda to Boston

Capitan Miranda

Plotting the inlets and reefs of the coast of Uruguay, the *Capitan Miranda*, now 80 years old, worked for four decades as a hydrographic vessel. Rescued from plans to break her up, she became a sail-training vessel for the Uruguayan navy. Her fine military band assures her popularity in European ports.

Asgard II

In Norse mythology, Asgard is the homeland of warrior gods. Her figurehead represents Grace O'Malley a notorious warrior, chieftain, noblewoman, gambler, mercenary and pirate queen of County Mayo in the 1500s.

Brilliant

Brilliant is nothing less than "one of the finest sailing vessels ever built, and a veteran of several Bermuda races and transatlantic voyages," says the American Sail Training Association's directory, *Sail Tall Ships*. Designed by brothers Rod and Olin Stephens of the famous American yacht firm Sparkman and Stephens in 1932, she competed often in the classic Newport-Bermuda race, and has made several transatlantic voyages.

Dar Mlodziezy (Poland)

The chief job of the *Dar Mlodziezy* is to train merchant navy officers. She mostly sails Baltic, European and American waters. Usually, she participates in one sail-training regatta per year, but four summers ago, she voyaged to Japan for Sail Osaka E697, and then made it all the way back to northern Europe for Cutty Sark Tall Ships' Races from Norway to Sweden. She is widely known as an excellent ship on which to throw parties.

Europa
The *Europa's* Tall Ships races usually last nine to 14 days. She has a busy European program but with as many as 50 paying passengers on board, she also undertakes the occasional worldwide voyage. Guests have their choice of two-, four- or six-berth cabins, each with ensuite showers and toilets, as well as roomy saloons and a big deckhouse.

Eye of the Wind
Though the *Eye of the Wind* is German-built and British-owned, her
heart and soul during Tall Ships 2000 was Canadian. Tall Ships
Millennium Challenge Inc., a non-profit organization in
Lunenburg, Nova Scotia, chartered her to enable hundreds of
young Canadians from all across the country to participate in what
corporation spokeswoman Karen Acton-Bond called "the maritime
event of the century."

Jens Krogh
One of the grand old ladies among Tall Ships, the 101-year-old *Jens Krogh* makes her gentle and stately way into dusk. "She is not an easy vessel to sail, and there are no wind instruments [to measure the speed and direction of the breeze]," Vice Admiral Sir George Vallings has written. "There are no winches to aid the hoisting or setting of sails, and the setting of top-sails in particular takes some know-how and can be fiddly....Downwind, *Jens Krogh* is a top-class, easy-to-handle racehorse...but going to windward she is something of an obstinate, underperforming donkey."

(OPPOSITE) The majestic bow of the *Irene* from the United Kingdom.

Lord Nelson
No Tall Ship afloat
is quite like the
Lord Nelson. She
boasts elevators
between decks;
flat, wide decks for
wheelchair users;
vibrator pads, fitted
to bunks, to alert
the hard-of-hearing
to emergencies;
equipment that
enables the hear-
ing-impaired to
thoroughly under-
stand briefings;
power steering to
allow weaker crew
to keep the ship on
course; Braille
markings; a
"speaking com-
pass" for blind
navigators; and, on
all voyages, a med-
ical purser and
doctor. Since her
maiden voyage 14
years ago, the *Lord
Nelson* has taken to
sea some 20,000
able-bodied and
disabled people.
They've ranged in
age from 16 to
those in their sev-
enties. Here, she
runs before the
wind, and into the
sunlight.

Morning Star of Revelation
Young crew of the *Morning Star* work as a team to hoist her big mainsail. Groups from churches, youth clubs and the disadvantaged, as well as outside organizations, cruise in the *Morning Star*.

Gorch Fock II
An officer of the German navy's sail-training ship *Gorch Fock II* bellows instructions to cadets unfurling sails far aloft. Named after a marine author famous in Germany, and affectionately known by her sailors as "Gofo," she entered her first Tall Ships race in 1960, and has been sailing the seven seas ever since. In 1999, she logged 38,000 nautical miles, visiting 18 ports in 16 nations on four continents.

Pogoria
A handsome, powerful 20-year-old, the steel-hulled *Pogoria* runs downwind.

(PREVIOUS PAGE)
Kruzenschtern
It was ships like this, built in the 1920s and the last of their kind, that inspired windjammer historian Alan Villiers to write, "Unlike steamships—squat, fat, smoking beasts, low with their stumpy masts and funnels—the *Cape Horner* was all ship. Your eye took in the whole of her with one sweeping look at her stirring stance....She was both strong and beautiful: power, grace and loveliness flowed in her lines from the curve of her seakindly cutwater to the harmony of her elegant stern."

Westward
Owned and operated by the Sea Education Association, the 29-year-old *Westward* is a sea-going classroom and scientific laboratory for "a variety of motivated and adventuresome students."

Tree of Life
Offering education in marine science, maritime history and tall ship handling, during the past seven years the *Tree of Life* has taught more than 200 trainees while completing her first voyage around the world. Before that, *Sail* magazine named her one of the top ten yachts in North America.

North American Race

Racing from Boston to Halifax, the Tall Ships 2000 fleet would be as big as it would get, and probably bigger than it has ever been before. Near the mouth of the Bay of Fundy, which separates Nova Scotia and New Brunswick and has the highest tides in the world, it was possible the vessels would face notoriously tricky combinations of strong currents, dense fogs and heavy seas. At Halifax, the capital of a province that's intensely proud of its seagoing history during war and peace, they could expect a welcome verging on ecstatic. Halifax has one of the finest natural harbors in the world. A city of little more than 300,000 people, it expected 750,000 visitors for the five days the Tall Ships would be berthed there.

Akogare
Completed by
Sumitomo Heavy
Industries in 1993,
Akogare was the
City of Osaka's
first sail-training
ship. The top fore-
sail of the forward
mast bears a sym-
bol that expresses
the philosophy of
the vessel, with the
sun rising, the
curve expressing
the strength of sail,
and the upward
arch signifying
human striving.
"A profound spiri-
tual strength and
the feeling of com-
passion towards
others," the ship's
document declares,
"are nurtured
through life togeth-
er on board such a
small world as a
ship."

Asgard II
Sailing on a summer breeze for the glory of the Emerald Isle.

Concordia
All is calm and all is under control aboard the barquentine that "takes the classroom to the world."

Dar Mlodziezy
Poland has a long history of sail training, and *Dar Mlodziezy* was once the nation's flagship. She's been a Tall Ships victor several times, and has a reputation for being fast and well-handled. Here, she's flying more than 20 sails.

Eendracht
Blessed by Queen
Beatrix when com-
missioned in 1989,
the *Eendracht*
("United We
Stand") sails
throughout the
year, from May to
November in
northern Europe,
and from
December to
April in the
Mediterranean and
around the
Canaries and
Azores. During
summer and
autumn holidays
she accepts only
15- to 25-year-old
trainees, but for
the rest of the year
she takes anyone
over 15. She
reserves 18 or so
days a year for Tall
Ships' races.

Europa
With two dozen sails set, the *Europa* sails comfortably before a light wind.

Irene
With every sail drawing, the workman-like but forever graceful *Irene* comes ploughing out of the past and into the summer of 2000.

The *Kaiwo Maru* of
Japan

Lord Nelson
With a fair wind behind them, and no shudder and stink of engine power, the crew of the *Lord Nelson* enjoy smooth sailing on the open Atlantic.

Kruzenschtern
Crewing aboard a Tall Ship requires, courage, strength, agility, teamwork, good humor and a strong sense of responsibility towards one's mates. Scenes like this delight the huge crowds that greet the ships at ports around the world.

Lettie G. Howard
Built 107 years ago at Essex, Massachusetts, the *Lettie G. Howard* may well be the oldest vessel participating in Tall Ships 2000. Here she's sailing wing-and-wing, with sails to both port and starboard. Schooners do that only when the wind is dead astern.

Oosterschelde

Big Dutch schooners once sailed all over the world. The *Oosterschelde*, built in 1918, worked the coasts of both Europe and Africa, carrying up to 400 tons of cargo, including included clay, bricks, bananas and salt herring. In the 1930s, she lost both her Dutch nationality and character as a Tall Ship. Her topmasts came down, and she gained a heavy diesel engine. She passed from Dutch hands to a Danish company, and then to a Swedish firm, which totally rebuilt her as a motor coaster.

In 1988, Dick van Andel bought her with plans to restore her as the last of the three-masted schooners that flew the Dutch flag a century ago. With fundraising from the Rotterdam Sailing Ship Foundation and expert counseling from three maritime museums, the costly work began in 1990. Two years later, Princess Margriet relaunched the vessel, and once again the *Oosterschelde* took to the ocean as a sailing ship.

82

Soren Larsen
Having appeared in the BBC TV series "The Onedin Line," the movie *The French Lieutenant's Woman* and a TV documentary about the Antarctic explorer, Sir Henry Ernest Shackleton, *Soren Larsen* is a celebrity among Tall Ships. Built in Denmark to carry coastal cargo around the north Atlantic and Baltic trading ports of Scandinavia, she was saved from destruction when, in 1978, the Davies family acquired her and faithfully restored her as a late nineteenth-century brigantine.

As the flagship for the Australian Bicentenary first Fleet Re-enactment Voyage in 1988, she led eight ships on a 22,000-mile trip from England to Sydney. She sailed to New Zealand to represent Britain in the anniversary celebrations of 1990, and returning to England via Cape Horn, she joined the 1992 transatlantic races that marked the Christopher Columbus centenary. She has sailed to pack ice beyond the Arctic Circle, and all through the hot, gorgeous islands of the South Pacific. The Davies family still owns her, and using Auckland, New Zealand, as her home port, she takes paying crew on adventure holidays to such exotic spots as Tonga, Fiji and New Caledonia.

Pogoria
Over placid waters, with all sails set, the *Pogoria* just ghosts along. Every day, each paying trainee serves a four-hour watch, takes eight hours off, and then reports for a "daywork" watch on which the main jobs involve cleaning the ship and helping out in the galley. During most on-watch hours, trainees keep the log up to date, serve as lookouts, trim sails and steer the ship. While going aloft is not compulsory, most want the thrill and experience of doing it.

Spirit of Massachusetts

The *Spirit of Massachusetts* was built in 1984, but in her beautiful design she is typical of the "fast and able" schooners out of Gloucester, Massachusetts, that generations ago fished the Grand Banks off Newfoundland and Georges Bank off New England and Nova Scotia. She sails primarily in the North Atlantic and the Caribbean Sea. The coed trainees, mostly young, learn about handling the ship, marine sciences, maritime history and ecology.

Tree of Life

Aboard the *Tree of Life*, all trainees share not only the ship handling, but the navigation, cooking and cleaning. Koa and teak grace her interior. Her spars are spruce, her deck is fir and all her varnished brightwork is Honduran mahogany. She can carry 4,500 square feet of sail and cruises at eight to 10 knots.

Eastward Transatlantic

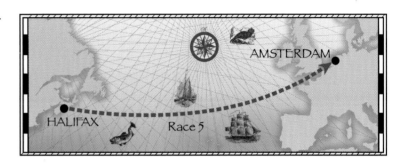

H aving made "the intellectu-
al discovery" of North
America in 1497, Italian
explorer John Cabot turned for
Europe "at the cape of the mainland
nearest to Ireland," and in his tubby
little caravel, the Matthew, zipped
across the Atlantic in only 15 days. Windjammer historian Alan Villiers
reported that in 1966, Argentina's fully rigged ship, the *Libertad*, with no
use of her engines, tore across the North Atlantic in only six days and 21
hours. But since North Atlantic weather can be unpredictable and most vessels participating in Tall Ships 2000 are much smaller than the *Libertad*,
planners allowed a full month for the race from Halifax to Amsterdam.

With its seventeenth century canals, ancient gabled houses, art galleries,
cafes, bars, antique shops, street markets and floating flower market,
Amsterdam is among the most intriguing and cosmopolitan cities in
Europe. Not only the Tall Ships, but hundreds of Dutch and foreign vessels,
from traditional Dutch flatbottoms to clippers, would honor Amsterdam's
centuries-old maritime heritage in a spectacular Parade of Sail. Tall Ships
2000 would end not with a bang, but with what it began: beauty.

Halifax to
Amsterdam

Akogare
The beauty of a barquentine rig, like that of the Japanese training
vessel *Akogare*, is that she gets some of the advantages of both
square-riggers and fore-and-afters. Here, even though the breeze is
hitting her starboard bow, she's slipping ahead.

Eendracht
The *Eendracht*, which encourages its young trainees to bring their musical instruments aboard, waltzes out to sea.

Oosterschelde
"Fare thee well,
Oosterschelde."
And to all the Tall
Ships, "Bon
Voyage!"

Gloria
Built at Bilboa, Spain, the *Gloria* was launched in 1969. During her frequent visits to
Europe, she makes a habit of entering harbors with her cadets far aloft manning her yards.

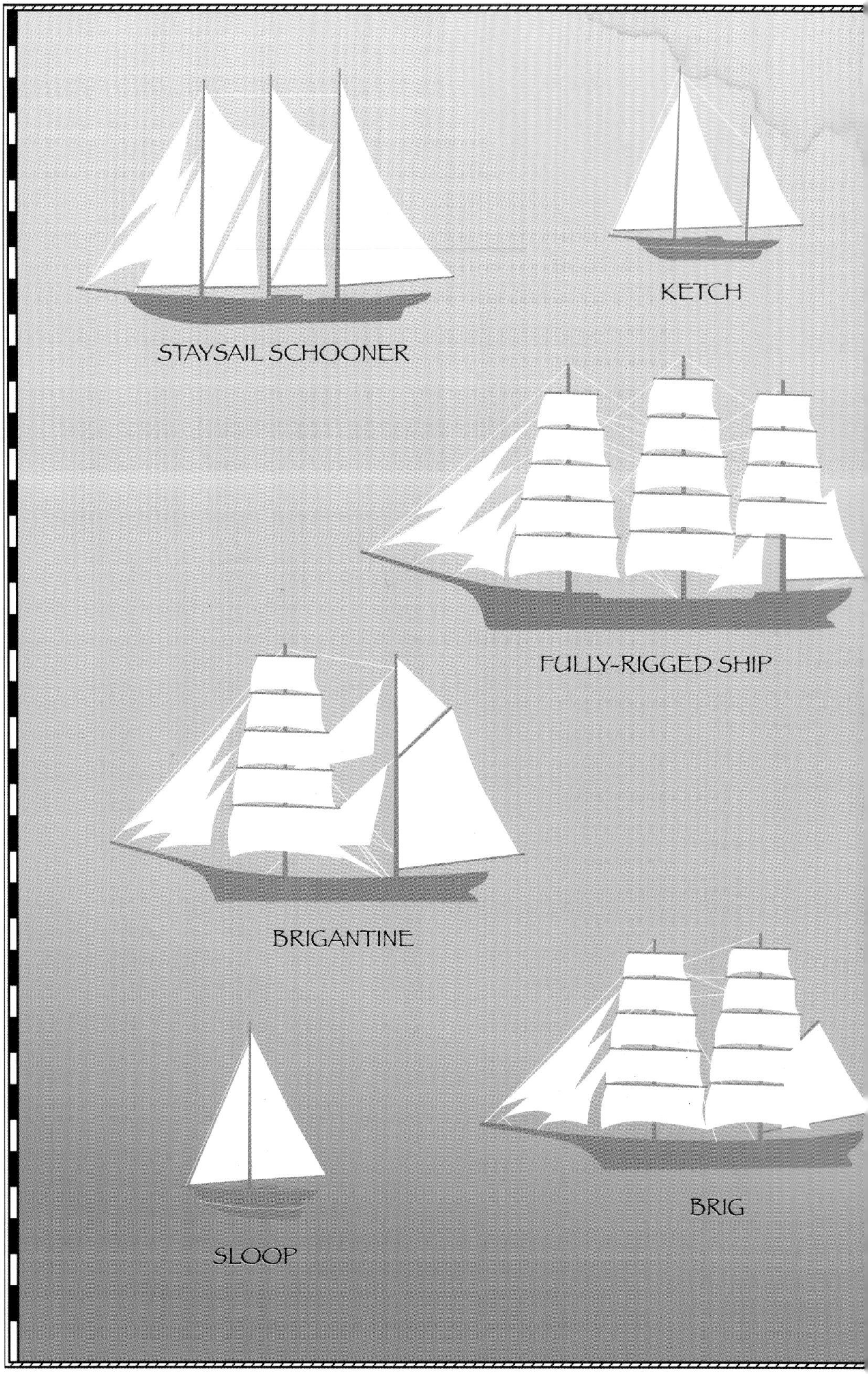

STAYSAIL SCHOONER

KETCH

FULLY-RIGGED SHIP

BRIGANTINE

BRIG

SLOOP

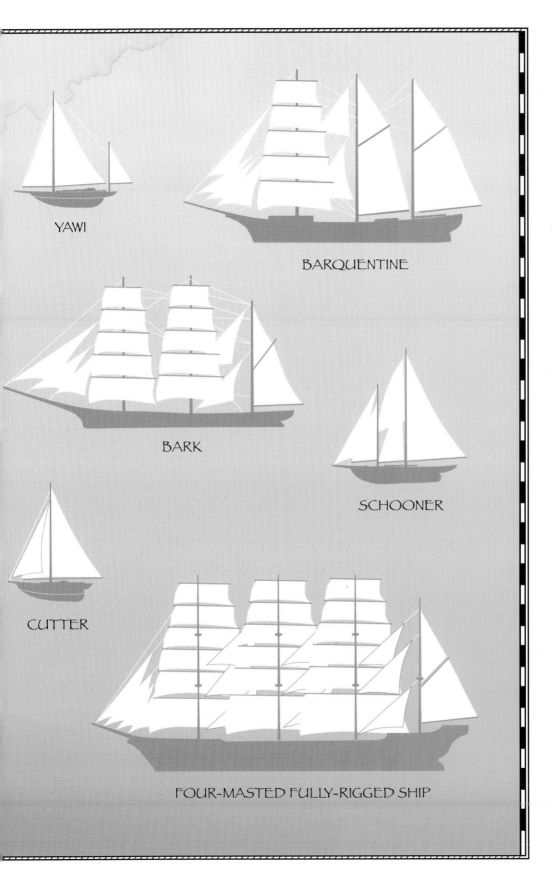

YAWI

BARQUENTINE

BARK

SCHOONER

CUTTER

FOUR-MASTED FULLY-RIGGED SHIP

The Classes

CLASS A
All square-rigged vessels with a length overall (LOA) of 120 feet (36.6 meters) or more, and all fore-and-aft rigged vessels with an LOA of 160 feet (48.8 meters) or more.

CLASS A Division II
All square-riggers with an LOA of less than 120 feet (36.6 meters). Square-riggers include fully rigged ships, barques, barquentines, brigs, brigantines.

CLASS B
Fore-and-aft rigged vessels with an LOA of between 100 feet (30.5 meters) and 160 feet (48.8 meters). Fore-and-afters include topsail schooners, schooners, ketches, yawls, cutters, sloops.

CLASS C
All other fore-and-aft rigged vessels with a waterline length of at least 30 feet (9.1 meters).
Class C Sub-classes:
Class I: gaff-rigged, under 100 feet (30.5 meters) (before 1939), no spinnaker.
Class II: Bermuda-rigged, under 100 feet (30.5 meters), no spinnaker.
Class III: All under 100 feet (30.5 meters), with spinnakers.

Note: LOA does not include a bowsprit, pulpit or any other extension of bow or stern. With respect to Class C and its sub-classes, a waterline of only 30 feet does not suggest a very tall ship, but the important qualification for any vessel to enter official Tall Ships Races is that at least half her crew be 16 to 25 years old. The chief purpose of the races is "to enable young people of all nations to race together at sea under sail."

Ship Specifications

Akogare (Japan)
Home port: Osaka. Rig: Barquentine. Length: 171 feet (52.1 meters). Crew: 12 professionals, 40 paying sail trainees.

Amerigo Vespucci (Italian Navy)
Home port: Unknown. Rig: Fully rigged ship. Length: 330 feet (100.6 meters). Crew: 240 officers, 120 men.

Asgard II (Ireland)
Home port: Dublin. Rig: Brigantine. Length: 106 feet (32.3 meters). Crew: 5 professionals, 20 paying trainees.

Bluenose II (Canada)
Home port: Lunenburg, Nova Scotia. Rig: Gaff topsail schooner. Length (including bowsprit): 191 feet (58.4 meters). Crew: 18 men and women.

Brilliant (USA)
Home port: Mystic Seaport, Connecticut. Rig: Gaff-rigged schooner. Length: Unknown. Crew: 3 for day trips and 4 for overnight voyages; 10 paying trainees for day sailing, 6 on overnight trips.

Capitan Miranda (Uruguay)
Home port: Unkown. Rig: Three-masted schooner. Length: 174 feet (53 meters). Crew: 102.

Concordia (Canada)
Home Port: Nassau, Bahamas. Rig: Unknown. Length: 188 feet (57.3 meters). Crew: 8 professionals, 8 trainees, 48 male and female students.

Dar Mlodziezy (Poland)
Home port: Gydnia. Rig: Fully rigged ship. Length: 358 feet (109.1 meters).Crew: 33 professionals, 20 fee-paying international trainees, 181 merchant navy cadets.

Eendracht (The Netherlands)
Home port: Scheveningen. Rig: Three-masted schooner. Length: 194 feet (59.1 meters). Crew: 13 or 14 professionals, 40 paying trainees.

Europa (The Netherlands)
Home port: Amsterdam. Rig: Three-masted barque. Length: 149 feet (45.4 meters). Crew: 9 professionals, 2 volunteers from the Dutch navy, up to 50 overnight paying sail trainees, or 100 trainees by day.

Gloria (Colombian Navy)
Home port: Unknown. Rig: barque. Length: 213 feet (65 meters). Crew: 10 officers, 88 trainees.

Eye of the Wind (United Kingdom)
Home Port: Faversham, Kent (southeast England). Rig: Brig. Length: 132 feet (40.2 meters). Crew: 9 professionals, 20 voyage crew.

Gorch Fock II (Germany)
Home port: Unknown. Rig: Barque. Length: 266 feet (81 meters). Crew (including cadets): 269.

Lettie G. Howard (USA)
Home port: New York City. Rig: Gaff topsail schooner. Length (including bowsprit): 129 feet (39.3 meters). Crew: 7 professional, 14 trainees.

Irene (USA)
Home Port: Unknown. Rig: Unknown. Length: Unknown. Crew: Unknown.

Jens Krogh (Denmark)
Home port: Aalborg. Rig: Gaff-rigged ketch. Length: 61 feet (18.6 meters). Crew: Paying skipper, two paying mates, 16 sail trainees.

Juan Sebastian de Elcano (Spanish Navy)
Home port: Unknown Rig. Four-masted schooner. Length: 305 feet (93 meters). Crew (including cadets): 95.

Kaliakra (Bulgaria)
Home port: Unknown. Rig: Barquentine. Length: 161 feet (49 meters). Crew: 21 permanent, 30 cadets.

Kruzenschtern (Russia)
Home port: Kaliningrad, Baltic Sea. Rig: Four-masted barque. Length: 372 feet (113.4 meters). Crew: 76 plus 202 cadets.

Lord Nelson (United Kingdom)
Home Port: Southampton. Rig: Three-masted barque. Length: 180 feet (55 meters). Crew: 8 professionals, 2 experienced volunteers, 40 paying sail trainees.

Morningstar of Revelation (United Kingdom)
Home port: Unknown. Rig: Ketch. Length: 62 feet (19 meters). Crew: Unknown.

Oosterschelde (The Netherlands)
Home port: Rotterdam. Rig: Three-masted schooner, with topsails on forward mast. Length: 164 feet (50 meters). Crew: 6 professionals, 36 paying sail trainees.

Pogoria (Poland)
Home port: Gydnia. Rig: Barquentine. Length: 157 feet (48 meters). Crew: 5 professionals, 5 volunteer officers, 38 paying sail trainees.

Rona II (United Kingdom)
Home port: Hamble, southern England. Rig: Yawl. Length: 68 feet (20.7 meters). Crew: 7 volunteers, 14 paying sail trainees.

Soren Larsen (United Kingdom)
Home port: Auckland, New Zealand. Rig: Brigantine. Length: 145 feet (44.2 meters). Crew: 12 professionals, 22 paying crew-passengers.

Spirit of Massachusetts (USA)
Home port: Boston. Rig: Gaff topsail schooner. Length (including bowsprit): 125 feet (38 meters). Crew: 7 professionals, 2 instructors, 50 paying trainees for daysails, 22 on overnight voyages.

Tree of Life (USA)
Home port: Alexandria, Virginia. Rig: Gaff schooner. Length (including bowsprit): 93 feet (28.3 meters). Crew: Unknown.

Westward (USA)
Home port: Woods Hole, Massachusetts. Rig: Staysail schooner. Length (including bowsprit): 125 feet (38 meters). Crew: 6 professional instructors, 24 student trainees.